itty-bitty Bible Activity Book

Noah's Ark

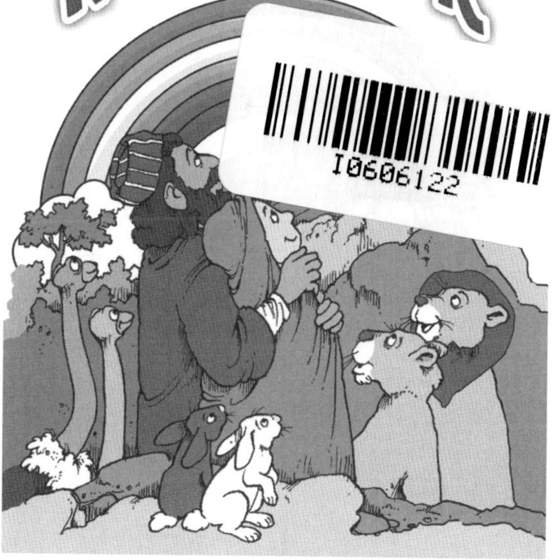

(Based on Genesis 6—9)

E4904

warnerpress®

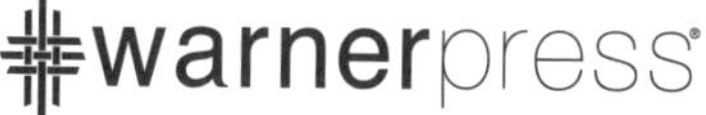

3058002100000270

People everywhere had become very wicked.
Only Noah and his sons obeyed God.

Find the hidden pictures:
hammer, saw, boat, lamb, Bible, apple, tack, fish

(ANSWERS ON PAGE 46)

God was sorry He had made people.
He decided to get rid of everything on earth and start over. But God was pleased with Noah.

What does the Bible say? Use the code to find out.

__ __ __ __   __ __ __ __ __
16 20 3 24   18 20 13 16 12

__ __ __ __ __   __ __
18 3 1 20 5   2 16

__ __ __   __ __ __ __
7 24 15   15 19 15 11

__ __   __ __ __
20 18   7 24 15

__ __ __ __ . Genesis 6:8 (NIV)
10 20 5 12

A	B	C	D	E	F	G	H	I	J	K	L	M
3	6	9	12	15	18	21	24	2	4	8	10	14

N	O	P	Q	R	S	T	U	V	W	X	Y	Z
16	20	22	26	5	11	7	13	1	17	25	19	23

(ANSWERS ON PAGE 46)

Noah loved God.

Connect the dots.

(ANSWERS ON PAGE 46)

Noah was a good man.
What does the Bible say about Noah?

Write the first letter of each picture in the boxes.

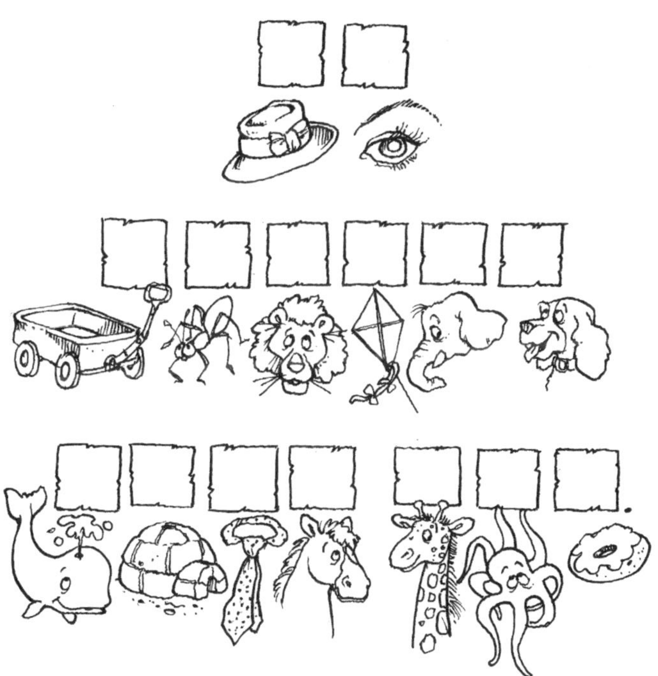

FROM GENESIS 6:9

(ANSWERS ON PAGE 46)

Noah had three sons.

What were their names? Write the letter that comes **BEFORE** the letters under the line to find out.

(ANSWERS ON PAGE 46)

God told Noah what He was going to do.
Then God said, "Noah, I want you to build an ark."

Color the picture.

So Noah did.

Connect the dots.

(ANSWERS ON PAGE 46)

God told Noah exactly how to build the ark.

Find and circle the words in the puzzle.

C U B I T S Z R S B P G I H A
Z P M E F E P K K N B N T R Z
K H D V V Y B N E T D U K D A
G I P H Q F B D H W E X U Y L
W P I P I H X W O Q R N S O C
A F T F J G L Z B O H E N J I
I W C L B N H K B K R G W C X
V A H K V R E K Z G I X A O G
R A Q W F X F W T Y D X K Q L
H O W D L L W O S F G Z N X B
W H O C E Y V D L N O T Q N O
A B H M K C H Q I O R E P P U
F K P X S Y K N H E L D D I M
O H N V F E E S V N W K A Q W
O X T T I P S D S S E R P Y C
R D R L O U W O O D D P R J Y

ARK	CYPRESS	WOOD	ROOMS
PITCH	CUBITS	LONG	WIDE
HIGH	ROOF	OPENING	DOOR
LOWER	MIDDLE	UPPER	DECKS

(ANSWERS ON PAGE 46)

What tools will Noah need?

Circle things he needs and put an **X** on things he doesn't.

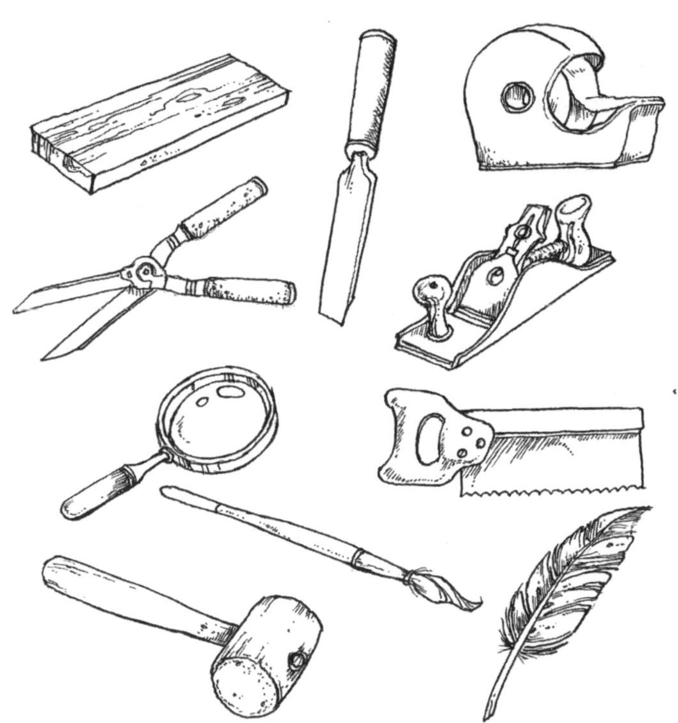

(ANSWERS ON PAGE 46)

Noah and his sons worked hard to build the ark just as God told them to do.

Put an **X** on **5** things that do not belong in the picture.

(ANSWERS ON PAGE 46)

Why did God want Noah to build an ark?

Write the letter on the line that comes **AFTER** the letter under the line.

(ANSWERS ON PAGE 46)

When the ark was ready, two of every kind of animal and bird came.

Draw your favorite animal and bird in the picture.

Find the name of each animal in the word bank.

Then write it next to the correct animal.

(ANSWERS ON PAGE 46)

A male and a female of each animal came to the ark.

Match the male and female animals.

(ANSWERS ON PAGE 46)

When the flood was over,
the animals would have babies again.

Match the baby animals to their mothers.

(ANSWERS ON PAGE 46)

Find and circle the animal names in the puzzle.

ELEPHANT	GIRAFFE	MOUSE
LION	DOG	HORSE
COW	TIGER	GOAT
ZEBRA	MONKEY	CAT

(ANSWERS ON PAGE 47)

God said, "Take all kinds of food for you and the animals to eat." So Noah did.

Write a **P** by the foods people eat.
Write an **A** by the animals' food.
Write a **B** by foods that both people and animals eat.

(ANSWERS ON PAGE 47)

The Bible says, "Noah did everything just as God commanded him" *(Genesis 6:22 NIV)*.

Write the underlined words in the grid where they fit.

(ANSWERS ON PAGE 47)

Finally, Noah and his wife along with his three sons and their wives all went into the ark.

Color the picture.

How old was Noah when God sent the flood to the earth?

Color in the spaces with dots to find out.

(ANSWERS ON PAGE 47)

When everyone was safely inside,
God shut the door of the ark.

Circle the hidden pictures: **rainbow, anchor, Bible, fish, cross, fishhook, umbrella, raincoat**

(ANSWERS ON PAGE 47)

Then the rain came pouring down. The water rose higher and higher until all the people and animals were washed away. Not one bit of dry ground was left.

Color the picture.

(ANSWERS ON PAGE 47)

How long did it rain?

Follow the lines from the letters to the boxes. Then write the letters to read the answer.

(ANSWERS ON PAGE 47)

The water covered the whole earth.
Not one living thing was left.

Find and circle the words in the puzzle.

S I I W P T Q U O I Q K N T B
H W G A R X T Q N H O W Z I X
B M A S E M X C P S K E R O L
A N A R L L O H H K G D W W U
A W D N M Q E R Y S S M P C Y
X W I I K R S E R U T A E R C
Q D Z L P I C M H H G U Q W O
Z N A Y D Z N F P N P Q A K E
Y F S E A A S D I M C W C Z H
R Z K D N F N H X F X O U L G
H O O H E B T I M K T D U S G
T F Q E A Y A S M S X S E O D
A O T U R X M V E A D J H I B
E U T E B B Q V X O L D E O D
R M V K O J I P V Q K S I V W
B E L O Q L Q J C E L P O E P

BIRDS	PEOPLE	EVERYTHING	LIVESTOCK
SWARM	BREATH	CREATURES	
DIED	MANKIND	WILD ANIMALS	

(ANSWERS ON PAGE 47)

God kept Noah, his family,
and all the animals safe inside the ark.

Color the picture.

High above the mountains, the ark floated on the water.

Find the path from the ark in the flood to the land.

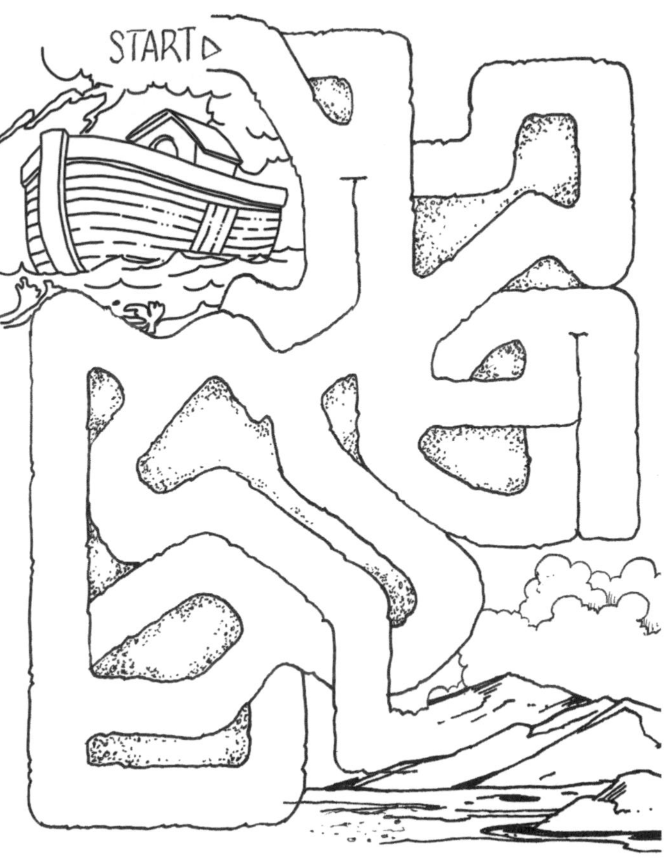

(ANSWERS ON PAGE 47)

How long did the water cover the land?

Trace the lines from the raindrops to the boxes they touch. Write the numbers or letters to read the answer.

(ANSWERS ON PAGE 47)

At last, the rain stopped.
God made the wind blow to dry up the water.

Color the picture.

Finally, the ark came to rest on a mountain.

Connect the dots.

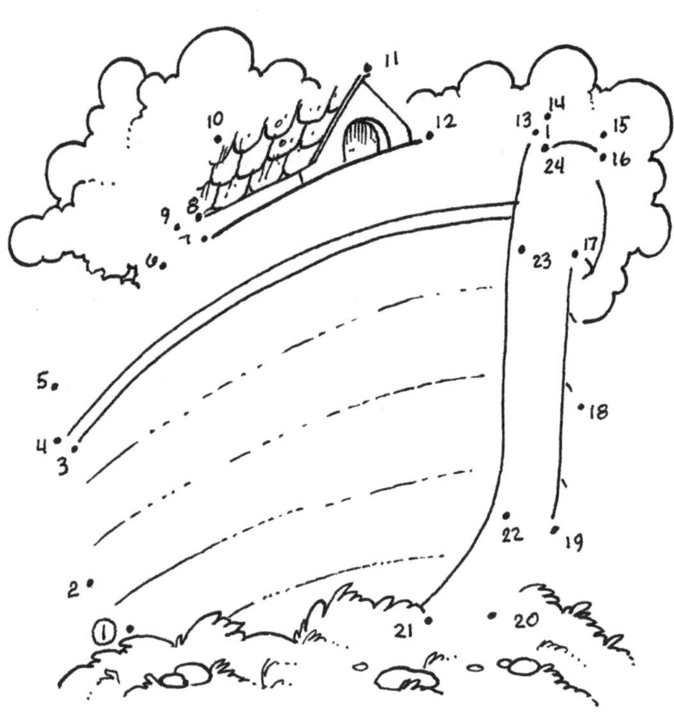

 (ANSWERS ON PAGE 47)

What was the name of the place where the ark came to rest?

Use the code to find out.

(ANSWERS ON PAGE 47)

After 40 days, Noah wanted to see what was happening. He opened a window and sent out a bird. It flew away and never came back.
What kind of bird was it?

Write the first letter of each picture to find out.

(ANSWERS ON PAGE 47)

Next, Noah said, "I will send out a dove to see if the ground is dry enough to live on." The dove came back because it could find no place to perch.

Color the picture.

Seven days later, Noah tried again. The dove flew and flew. At last, it found an olive tree.

Help the dove find the olive tree.

(ANSWERS ON PAGE 47)

The dove took a leaf from the olive tree back to Noah.

Color the picture.

Finally, the earth was completely dry. God spoke to Noah. What did He say?

Write the letter that comes **BEFORE** the letter under each line to find out.

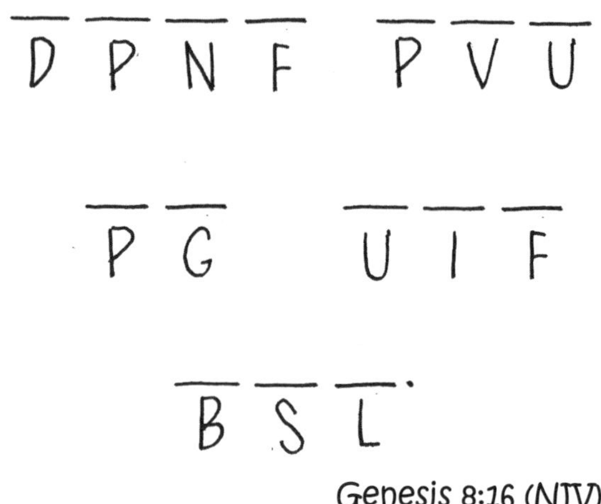

ABCDEFGHIJKLM
NOPQRSTUVWXYZ

(ANSWERS ON PAGE 47)

Noah, his family, and all the animals came out of the ark.

Circle the hidden pictures: **cross, bell, lightning bolt, candle, umbrella, heart, star, fish**

(ANSWERS ON PAGE 48)

Noah must have been very happy to see dry land again! What was the first thing he did?

Use the code to find out.

16 20 3 24   6 13 2 10 7

3 16   3 10 7 3 5

7 20   7 24 15

10 20 5 12 . Genesis 8:20 (NIV)

A	B	C	D	E	F	G	H	I	J	K	L	M
3	6	9	12	15	18	21	24	2	4	8	10	14
N	O	P	Q	R	S	T	U	V	W	X	Y	Z
16	20	22	26	5	11	7	13	1	17	25	19	23

(ANSWERS ON PAGE 48)

God was pleased with Noah's offering.
What did God say?

Use the word bank to fill in the blanks.

day	heat	earth	night
winter	summer	harvest	seedtime

As long as the ____ ____ ____ ____ ____ endures,

____ ____ ____ ____ ____ ____ ____ ____

and ____ ____ ____ ____ ____ ____ ____,

cold and ____ ____ ____ ____,

____ ____ ____ ____ ____ ____ and

____ ____ ____ ____ ____ ____, ____ ____ ____

and ____ ____ ____ ____ ____

will never cease. Genesis 8:22 (NIV)

(ANSWERS ON PAGE 48)

God made a covenant with Noah. What was it?

Match the numbers under the lines to letters on the ship's wheel to read the Bible verse.

N A V I Y F T D W S O L E R G U

1 2 3 4 5 6 7 8 9 10 11 12 13 14 15 16

1 13 3 13 14

2 15 2 4 1

WILL 2 12 12 12 4 6 13 BE

8 13 10 7 14 11 5 13 8

BY THE 9 2 7 13 14 10 OF A

6 12 11 11 8.

Genesis 9:11 (NIV)

(ANSWERS ON PAGE 48)

What did God put in the sky as a reminder of His promise?

Connect the dots.

(ANSWERS ON PAGE 48)

God said, "Whenever the rainbow appears in the clouds, I will see it and remember the everlasting covenant between God and all living creatures" *(Genesis 9:16 NIV).*

Write the underlined words in the grid where they fit.

(ANSWERS ON PAGE 48)

Put an **X** on **8** objects that do not belong in the picture.

(ANSWERS ON PAGE 48)

Noah lived another 350 years after the flood was over. How old was he when he died?

Color in the spaces with dots to find out.

(ANSWERS ON PAGE 48)

Draw a picture of your favorite animal.

Page 2

Page 3

Noah found favor in the eyes of the Lord.

Page 4

Page 5

He walked with God.

Page 6

Shem, Ham & Japheth

Page 8

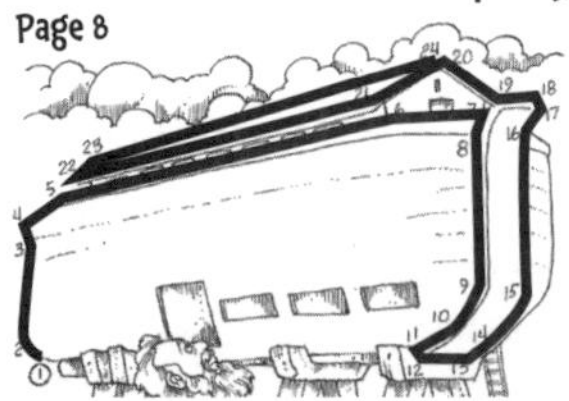

Page 9

Page 10

Page 11

Page 12

God was sending a flood to cover the earth.

Page 14

Page 15

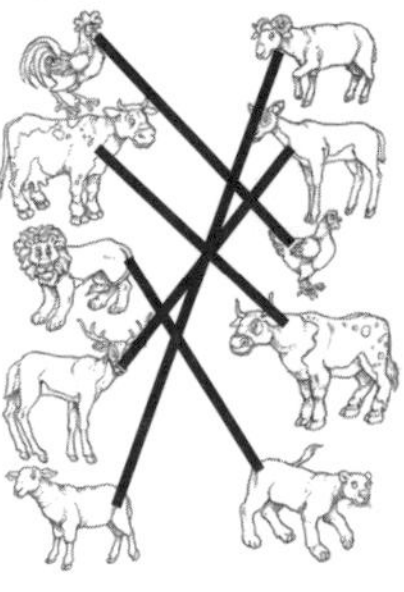

Page 16

Page 17

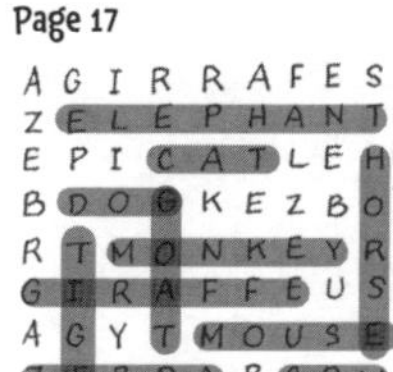

Page 18

Page 19

Page 21

Page 22

Page 24

Forty days and forty nights.

Page 25

Page 27

Page 28

150 Days

Page 30

Page 31

The mountains of Ararat

Page 32

A Raven

Page 34

Page 36

Come out of the ark.

Page 37

Page 38

Noah built an altar to the Lord.

Page 39

"As long as the **earth** endures, **seedtime** and **harvest**, cold and **heat**, **summer** and **winter**,**day** and **night** will never cease."

Page 40

Never again will all life be destroyed by the waters of a flood.

Page 41

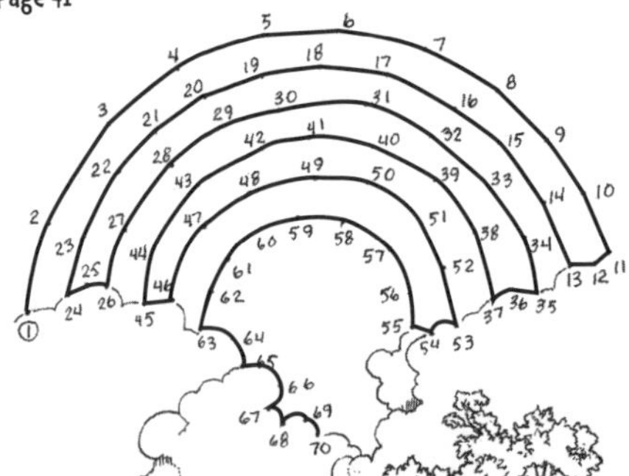

Page 42

					C						
A	P	P	E	A	R	S			R		
			V		E				E		
C	O	V	E	N	A	N	T		M		
L			R		T				E		
O			L		U		L		M		
U			A		R	A	I	N	B	O	W
D			S	E	E		V		E		
S			T		S		I		R		
			I				N				
			N				G				
			G	O	D						

Page 43

Page 44

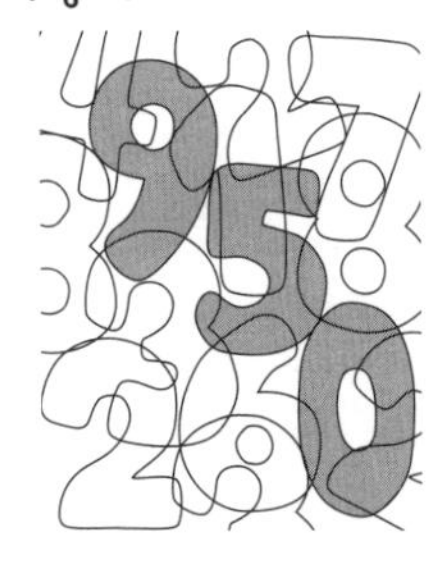